MACHINES ON THE MOVE

SUBMARINES

Andrew Langley

amicus

Published by Amicus
P.O. Box 1329
Mankato, MN 56002

Printed in the United States of America, at Corporate Graphics in North Mankato, Minnesota.

Library of Congress Cataloging-in-Publication Data
Langley, Andrew.
  Submarines / by Andrew Langley.
      p. cm. – (Machines on the move)
  Includes index.
  ISBN 978-1-60753-062-6 (library binding)
  1. Submarines (Ships)–Juvenile literature. I. Title.
  VM365.L24 2011
  623.82'05–dc22

                              2010006435

Planning and production by Discovery Books Limited
Designed by D.R. ink
Cover design by Blink Media
Edited by James Nixon

Photograph acknowledgements
BAE Systems: pp. 23 bottom, 29; Corbis: pp. 18 (Roger Ressmeyer), 19 middle (Steve Kaufman); Getty Images: pp. 4 (BAE Systems), 7 (J. Baylor Roberts/National Geographic), 8 (BAE Systems), 10 bottom (Toru Yamanaka/ AFP), 13, 24 (Bates Littlehales/National Geographic), 25 top (Stephen Frink/The Image Bank), 25 bottom (Keystone); Kockums AB: p. 9 top; NOAA Photo Library: p. 27 top (R. Wickland/OAR/National Undersea Research Program); Picasa Web: p. 9 bottom (Kobus); Royal Navy: p. 23 middle (© Crown Copyright/MOD, image from www.photos.mod.uk. Reproduced with the permission of the Controller of Her Majesty's Stationery Office); Shutterstock: pp. 12 (Danilo Ducak), 15 top (Jens Stolt), 19 middle (Valeriy Velikov); US Navy: pp. 6, 7 top, 10 top, 11, 14, 16, 17 bottom, 20, 21, 22, 23 top, 26, 27 bottom, 28; Wikimedia: pp. 5 bottom (Geni), 13 top (Clem Rutter), 19 bottom (Broken Sphere).

Front cover: Kockums AB: top;
US Navy: bottom

DAD0042
32010

9 8 7 6 5 4 3 2 1

Contents

What Is a Submarine?

A submarine is a boat that can travel underwater and on top of the water. It can stay underwater for many days.

Most submarines are made for fighting in times of war. They attack enemy ships and fire **missiles**. Other submarines are used for peaceful jobs, such as exploring the seafloor.

Parts of a Submarine

Sail: platform with antennas and scopes

Rudder: steers the submarine right or left

Propeller: pushes the submarine along

Torpedo Tubes: for firing torpedoes

Hull: the main body of the boat

Diving Planes: direct the submarine up or down

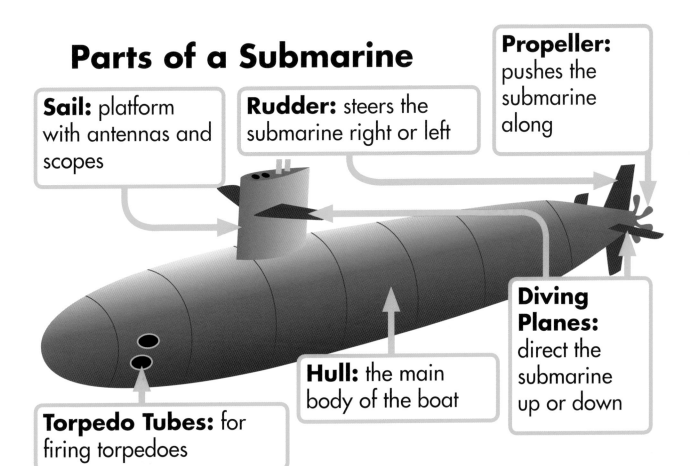

Pedal-Powered Sub

One of the first submarines was made of wood. The *Turtle*, built in 1775, held one man, who had to steer and pedal the tiny craft along.

In the Control Room

The control room is in the center of the submarine. Two members of the crew use controls to adjust the **rudder** and **diving planes**. These steer and direct the submarine.

Helmsman: controls the rudder

Planesman: adjusts the diving planes

A submarine does not move like an ordinary ship, but more like an aircraft. It can travel up or down, as well as from side to side.

Planes

The sub has two planes mounted near the **propeller**, and two more on the sail. These are like the flaps of an aircraft. They can be moved to direct the sub upward or downward.

Plane

Subs with Weapons

There are two main types of submarines. An attack submarine finds and destroys other ships. A **ballistic missile** submarine fires long-range missiles that can destroy targets on land or at sea. These weapons are launched using a control panel (above) in the control room.

Driving Force

Designers of subs have a big problem. Most ordinary engines work using oxygen from the air. But there is no air underwater.

Many modern subs have electric engines powered by **nuclear energy**. These engines do not need air.

Nuclear Engine

A nuclear engine uses power from a material called **uranium**. This produces a lot of heat that boils water into steam. The steam drives a **generator**, which, in turn, makes electrical power.

Some subs use **diesel engines** when they are on the surface (right). When they dive, they switch to electric engines, which do not need oxygen from the air.

Speediest Submarine

The fastest-ever submarine was the Russian K-222, launched in 1969. Its nuclear engine pushed it to speeds of more than 50 miles (80 km) per hour.

Diving and Surfacing

A submarine has **ballast** tanks at both ends. These are used for making the sub dive under the water and rise to the surface again.

Submarine Diving

For diving, the tanks at each end are opened so that they fill with seawater. This makes the ship heavier, so it sinks.

Submarine Surfacing

To surface, the water is forced out of the tanks. This makes the sub lighter, so it rises again.

Ballast Tanks

There are two kinds of ballast tanks. The main tanks are used for diving or surfacing. Smaller tanks are filled or emptied underwater. Small tanks help control the depth at which the submarine travels.

Under the Ice

Nuclear submarines can even travel right under the North Pole. They sometimes surface through thin patches of ice.

Torpedoes and Missiles

The main job of military submarines is to attack enemies at sea and on land.

Attack submarines fire **torpedoes** from special tubes. The torpedoes explode when they hit another ship.

Torpedo

Missile Silo

Missile Silos

Missiles are stored in tubes called **silos**. They can be launched underwater. Once they are out of the water, their rocket motors start.

Lying in Wait

Missile submarines launch high-powered missiles that can hit enemy targets over 3,728 miles (6,000 km) away. Ballistic missile submarines patrol near the coasts of enemy countries. They can hide under the surface for as long as six months!

The Silent Deep

Submarines can be attacked by other ships, aircraft, or missiles. They try to avoid being spotted from above or below the surface.

Submarines hide by only coming to the surface very rarely. Modern sensing equipment on warships can easily pick up sounds underwater. A submarine must be as quiet as possible.

Propeller

The propeller is specially designed to push the sub along at high speeds but make very little noise.

Pump Jets

Some subs have no propellers at all. Instead, they propel themselves forward with pump jets, which force out a stream of high-pressure water. These are much quieter than turning propellers.

Using Signals

A submarine has to keep the right course and avoid hidden obstacles. To find their way, the crew uses signals from **satellites** in space and onboard computers that keep track of the sub's movements.

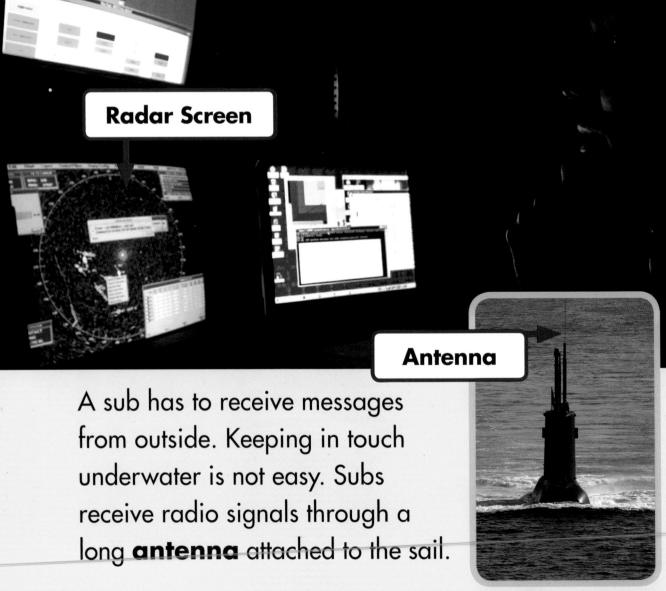

Radar Screen

Antenna

A sub has to receive messages from outside. Keeping in touch underwater is not easy. Subs receive radio signals through a long **antenna** attached to the sail.

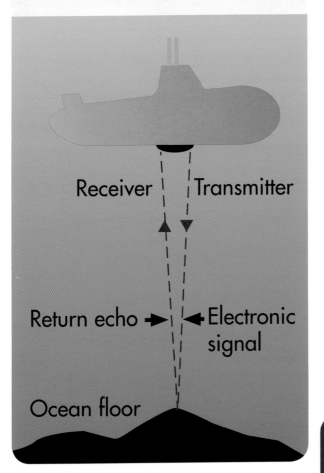

Receiver | Transmitter

Return echo → ← Electronic signal

Ocean floor

Echo Sounder

An echo sounder bounces electronic signals off the seafloor, which "echo" back to the sub (left). The machine can tell how close the sub is to the seafloor by timing how quickly the echo returns.

Up Periscope!

The periscope is a tube that can be raised above the water. It allows the crew to see what is happening on the surface when the sub is underwater.

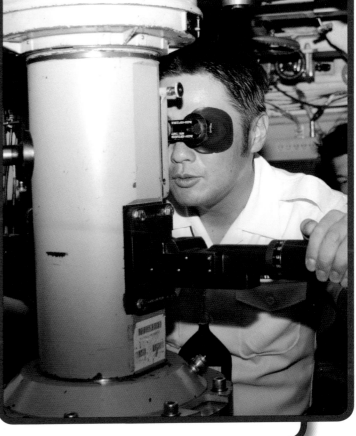

Living Underwater

The crew of a submarine needs a constant supply of fresh air and fresh water. Filters remove harmful gases from the air that the crew breathes out. Meanwhile, new supplies of oxygen are taken out from the seawater.

Air Monitor

A special system keeps the air healthy on board. It checks samples from all parts of the sub and removes any poisonous gases.

Submarines can make their own fresh water—even deep under the sea. Clean drinking water is made from seawater.

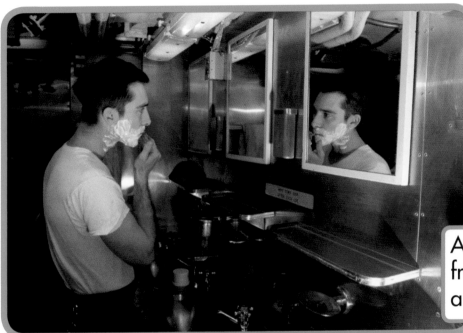

A crew member using freshwater on board a submarine.

Evaporator

This machine boils seawater, leaving the salt behind. It then collects the steam and turns it back into pure water, which is ready for drinking.

Evaporator

Daily Life

Big nuclear submarines, such as a ballistic missile carrier, have as many as 150 people on board. Smaller subs may have 80 people or fewer.

Video Screen

Life underwater can be difficult. The crew is cut off from the outside world for long periods. But submarines have many comforts, including good food, entertainment centers, and exercise rooms.

Staying Underwater

The fuel in a modern nuclear sub lasts for about five years. All this time, the sub could keep producing fresh air and water. The only thing that would run out is food.

Throwing Out Garbage

All the garbage on board is squashed into steel cans. Then the cans are dropped out through special tubes and fall onto the seafloor.

Emergency!

The deep sea is a very dangerous place —even if you're inside a huge metal tube. A small accident can quickly become a disaster.

A submarine crew is trained to deal with problems, such as leaks and fires. In the worst case, the crew will have to escape from the sub and swim to the surface.

Submarine Escape Suit

Escape Trunk

In an emergency, the crew can leave the ship through a small chamber called the escape trunk (right). They shut themselves in the chamber and fill it with seawater. Then they open the outer **hatch** and swim out.

Search and Rescue

Special rescue crafts are sent down to submarines that have sunk. They can connect up with the sub's escape hatches and rescue trapped crew members.

Exploring the Deep

Parts of the ocean are very deep—as deep as Mount Everest is high. Only a special type of submarine called a submersible can go to these depths.

Submersibles are small but strong. Most are attached by cables to ships on the surface. They have explored the deepest parts of the sea, and have discovered many amazing things, such as rare fish and shipwrecks.

Hull

Submersible Hull

A submersible has a very strong **hull** with thick walls. They need them to stop the sub from being squashed by the weight of water at great depths.

Deepest-Ever Dive

Only one craft has ever visited the deepest part of the ocean, more than 6.8 miles (11,000 m) down. This was the *Trieste* in 1960. The journey down took five hours.

One-Man Subs

Not all submarines are large and powerful. Some are very small, big enough for only one person.

One of the smallest subs is the Newt diving suit. This is a submarine you can wear! Made of aluminum, it has joints so divers can bend their arms and legs.

Newt Suit

The Newt suit is powered by propellers and water jets that push it through the water.

Robot Arms

Many diving suits have arms that are powered by the diver. The arms have grippers at the end, which can be used for many jobs, from cutting and drilling to taking photos.

Gripper

Remote-Controlled Subs

Some small submarines have no crew at all. Remotely Operated Vehicles (ROVs) are controlled from the surface. ROVs are used to inspect underwater pipelines and cables.

Future Submarines

Submarines are some of the most important ships used in the **Navy**. What could they look like in the future?

Future subs will have more weapons. The new USS *Ohio* (below) can carry and launch up to 154 torpedoes!

Quieter Engines

Scientists are developing quieter kinds of engines. These use liquids such as seawater instead of a propeller. Magnets and electric currents force the seawater out behind the boat, pushing it along.

Electronic systems will do many of the jobs done by humans. This means that future subs will be smaller, because they will need a smaller crew. A lot of submarines will be **remote-controlled**, with no crew at all. They will be able to stay hidden underwater for much longer periods.

This tiny, remote-controlled sub is called *Talisman L.* It has been developed to detect and deal with explosive **mines**.

Glossary

antenna used for receiving radio signals

ballast a heavy material (such as seawater) used to make a submarine dive

ballistic missile a missile that is sent into the air by rocket power and then falls freely onto its target

diesel engine an engine that burns diesel oil as a fuel

diving planes the fins attached to the side of a sub, which direct the boat up or down

evaporator a machine that heats seawater so that it turns into vapor. The vapor is then turned into drinking water.

generator a machine that turns movement into electrical energy

hatch the door covering an opening in the hull

hull the main body of a submarine or other ship

mine a type of bomb placed under the water

missile a weapon that is thrown or fired at a target

navy the ships and people that defend a country at sea

nuclear energy energy released by the splitting of very small parts (atoms) of the metal uranium

oxygen a common gas in the air that is needed for human life and for some kinds of engines

periscope an instrument made of a tube and mirrors that allows someone to see something that is out of their line of sight

propeller a set of spinning blades that drive a boat forward

remote-controlled when the movement of something is directed from a distant point

rudder a hinged plate at the back of a boat used for steering

satellite a man-made object that flies around the Earth in space, sending out radio signals

silo a long cylinder-shaped structure for storing missiles

submersible a small boat with very thick walls that can operate underwater at great depths

torpedo a tube-shaped weapon launched through the water from a submarine or other boat

uranium a kind of metal used to produce nuclear energy

Index

Web Sites

www.navy.mil/navydata/ships/subs/subs.asp
Descriptions of submarines in the U.S. Navy fleet.

www.navy.mil/navydata/cno/n87/faq.html
Answers to the most common submarine questions.

http://science.howstuffworks.com/nuclear-submarine5.htm
Find out how nuclear submarines work.